PRECIOUS METALS INVESTING

FOR BEGINNERS

THE QUICK GUIDE TO PLATINUM AND PALLADIUM

ALEX NKENCHOR UWAJEH

Precious Metals Investing For Beginners: The Quick Guide to Platinum and Palladium

By

Alex Nkenchor Uwajeh

Legal Notice:

This book covers the basics and also what you need to know about investing in platinum and palladium. It presents a brief history and background on the precious metals, platinum and palladium, covering some definitions and continuing on about mining, exploration and risks involved in the industry as well as how the investment strategy works. This book also differentiates advantages and disadvantages of investing in platinum and palladium, for example, as an investment for growth and an investment for income purposes.

Platinum and Palladium: An Introduction

Platinum and palladium are designated both as precious and industrial metals. Similar to gold these two metals have value even in small amounts. Both metals are in high demand for use in electronics, dentistry and catalytic converters for the automobile industry. Like gold, platinum and palladium have had their highs and lows. In 2007 platinum was $2,000 an ounce, and the price was predicted to climb due to platinum's relative rarity. Palladium is even rarer and its value is matching platinum's on the commodities market.

Demand is continuously increasing for these two metals, but supply and production is in short supply. More than 90% of the world's stores of platinum and palladium are located in South Africa and Russia and there are only a handful of platinum mining companies in the world. The largest platinum and palladium mining company is Stillwater Mining Company located in Montana, United States.

It is the only producer of platinum and palladium in the United States. Investors, commodities and precious metal markets watch the listing on Stillwater's profile to determine price fluctuations of these two precious metals.

Ongoing labor strikes in South Africa are definite problems for the platinum and palladium markets. The car muffler industry depends on these metals for use in their catalytic converters and electronics, dental and pharmaceutical industries look to palladium for alloy stabilization. Prices for an ounce of platinum have surged to just under $1500 and palladium is experiencing prices of $850 an ounce. In addition to high prices, these two precious metals have been listed on the supply risk index at number thirteen.

Greater shortages loom in the very near future. South Africa and Russian the two suppliers of platinum and palladium are experiencing economic hardships. South Africa is having intense strikes and labor issues while Russia is experiencing economic sanctions due to their part in the Ukraine rebellion.

Platinum

Platinum was first discovered by Julius Scaliger in 1735. The first tailings were found in the alluvial sands of South American rivers. Platinum is named after the Spanish word platina or little silver. It is colored a silvery-white and will not oxidize in air at any temperature.

Scientifically, platinum is distinguished by the atomic number of 78 and is listed in the same periodic table as nickel. Six isotopes distinguish platinum: These include platinum-194, platinum-195, platinum 196, platinum 198 and platinum 12 plus platinum-190 or the weakly radioactive portion of platinum (http://www.lenntech.com/periodic/elements/pt.htm).

Platinum has high resistance to corrosion and can withstand high temperatures without melting. It is considered a noble metal, or a metal that resists oxidation and corrosion. Pure platinum is malleable and ductile and often confused with silver. It is one of the most ductile metals, or has a high ability to deform under tensile stress. Platinum is also measured by malleability or a measurement of by how well a metal changes under compressive stress. Compressive stress includes forming metals into sheets by stretching and rolling without fracturing. Ductile metals easily stretch into wires and can be wrapped around different substances to make industrial products or jewelry.

Platinum is a bit harder than pure iron and is highly resistant to corrosion, is stable at high temperatures and is excellent in electrical products. Because of the characteristics of ductibility or deforming and malleability, platinum is highly sought after for industrial and electrical applications. High resistance to wear and tarnish makes platinum perfect for fine jewelry.

Platinum in addition to its known alloys are utilized in laboratory apparatus, electrical contact points, electrical resistance wires, and surgical tools. Catalytic converters are 30 percent platinum. The glass industry uses platinum in liquid crystal display glass and optical fibers. Your laptop screen probably has platinum alloys.

Platinum occurs naturally within basic igneous rocks. Three-quarters of the world's platinum is mined in South Africa. Russia is the second largest producer and North America is third largest producer of platinum with mines in Montana and Canada. There are currently more than 30.000 tons of platinum in reserve and platinum mining produces about 155 tons a year.

Platinum is a very safe metal. Concentrations of platinum in soils are minimal and platinum bonds are safe enough to be applied as medicine in cancer cures. The level of healing properties in platinum depends on the bonding, exposure and immunity levels of treated persons.

Palladium

Palladium is a very rare and steel-white metal first discovered in 1803 by William Hyde Wollaston. In addition to palladium, platinum, iridium, rhodium and osmium form a group of metals known as the platinum group of metals or PGM. Palladium has a lower melting point than platinum and is lower in density than most of PGM. Stores of palladium can be found in cooperite and polarite, rare minerals requiring mining and complex processing to extract the palladium. Geologically palladium is known by the chemical symbol of PD and is the 46th element in the periodic table. It has similar malleability as does platinum and palladium becomes stronger and harder after cold work.

Palladium bears the distinction of being the least dense and lowest melting point of the PGM (platinum group metals). Palladium absorbs up to 900 times its own volume of hydrogen. Hydrogen diffuses through heated palladium in petroleum applications and catalytic converters and this diffusion purifies dangerous automobile emissions.

In 1903 William Hyde Wollaston named palladium after the asteroid "pallas" which was discovered in the same year. Wollaston found palladium in crude platinum ore from South America. He dissolved platinum ore in aqua regia (hydrochloric and nitric acids) neutralized the acid with sodium hydroxide and further treated platinum with ammonium chloride. Palladium was removed and the metal as produced by cyanide and heating.

The extraction of palladium is often the main focus of industrial refinement operations and at other times it is a natural by product of ore refining. Extraction of palladium is complex but the need for palladium far outweighs the cost.

Palladium is refined for use in the automobile industry – specifically catalytic converters. These converters replace 90% of damaging gases from auto exhaust into substances that follow governmental pollution guidelines. Palladium is important for making crowns for the dental industry, electronics, hydrogen purification and medicine. This metal is used in fuel cell technology to produce electricity, purify water and generate heat. Multilayer capacitors use palladium and palladium alloys for electrodes. When alloyed with nickel, palladium is important in connector plating for consumer electronics.

Experiments prove palladium can be produced in small numbers in nuclear fission reactors. However the technology for this type of extraction is still in the experimental stages.

Palladium components are also used in a new composite of metallic glass. Called DH3 and currently in development by the California Institute of Technology, palladium's high bulk to shear ratio is as tough as steel. Medical advances use palladium nanoparticles to move drug to precise locations inside the body.

Deposits of palladium are somewhat rare with the most extensive deposits found in Bushveld Igneous Complex in South Africa, The Stillwater Complex in Montana, the Thunder Bay District of Ontario, Canada, and large deposits in the Norilsk Complex in Russia.

Mining, Exploration and Risk

Exploration

Finding palladium and platinum, rare metals high in demand for the chemical, pharmaceutical and automobile industries, is difficult and time consuming. Platinum heavy ores exist in basic rocks that are rich in iron, chrome and nickel. These ores were formed via a natural process from molten rock as it cooled in the earth. Platinum ores are never present in quartz veins. Platinum can be found in small amounts in copper ores.

The pharmacology research department of the University of Pittsburgh has developed an easy, quick and inexpensive method of discovering palladium/platinum deposits for the production of pharmaceuticals. It is a basic fluorescein-based solution that glows green when any amount of palladium and platinum is found. This method takes only one hour which is a far cry from the days-long and tedious traditional technology. Scientists proclaim that this team's method can be used on mining sites and platinum mining companies are exploring the possibilities.

Platinum and palladium are scarce and noble metals obtained by extracting and refining specific ore supplies. Exploration discovered palladium and platinum in Russia, South Africa, and areas of North America in primary deposits and placers. Deposits are found in local concentrations of olivine-rich rock or dunite. Palladium can also be found in chromite, native platinum and iridosmine. Erosion in ore beds exposes deposits of the platinum-quality metals. A second supply of platinum and palladium comes from come from nickel-copper sulphide associated with norite or granular igneous rocks containing light and dark minerals. These minerals are calcic plagioclase feldspars and orthorhombic pyroxenes.

Mining and producing platinum and palladium is investment resource intensive. Large capital expenditures are needed to build production facilities, finance exploration and production. Ores known to contain the elements of platinum and palladium are processed through complicated milling, flotation and smelting. These production techniques aim to produce a matte that contains platinum group metals and most mines do on-site processing. Further refining takes place when the metals are shipped to other refineries.

Mining

Platinum and palladium mining companies have different ways to deal with refining, fabricating, assaying, researching and trading. All methods of assaying, developing, mining and refining take over six months to complete. Almost 12 tons of ore is needed to produce one ounce of platinum. Palladium takes much more ore to produce a single ounce and extraction and refining processes are more time consuming.

Stillwater Mining Company in Montana is heavily occupied in the extraction, exploration and refining of palladium and platinum. Stillwater extracts platinum and palladium from the Stillwater igneous compound which is recognized as the J-M Reef. The J-M Reef is narrow but has a strike length of over 28 miles. Stillwater is also involved in the reprocessing of used catalytic converters.

The majority of ore mined to produce platinum and palladium metals comes from mechanized ramp and fill mining techniques, sub-level stoping, and slushier cut and fill. When the ore body is close to the surface, platinum and palladium can be mined in open pit techniques. Open pit is the most cost effective methods of extracting platinum/palladium rich ore. Open pit mining is almost 40 percent less in cost than conventional mining methods and is much safer than underground mining. (http://www.palladiumcoins.com/mining.html) .

- Ramp and fill mining begins on a straight stope and miners use drills, either handheld or mechanized for making blasting holes. High load-haul-dump mucking machines haul away the ore. Stoping extracts the ore from underground levels and leaves behind open spaces. These open spaces are backfilled with rock and stone and form the stopes. If the backfill is strong enough and no cave- ins occur, this method is highly productive.

Cuts in the stope are made in 9-foot increments with the ground being artificially supported with rock bolts and other mining materials. When the stope is fully mined it is backfilled with waste rock and sand. This is the floor for the next horizontal stope.

As a note, in mining terms, stoping is considered productive or ongoing. Mining platinum and palladium is productive as opposed to deadwork or preparatory mining.

- Sub-level stoping uses a ramp along the footwall of a reef. This allows access to the ore at 50 foot vertical intervals. Long-hole drilling and blasting methods are used to remove the earth between two sublevels. The length of the opening can be up to 100 feet along the strike. The length a level is mined is dependent on ore deposits and ground stability. Removing ore from open stopes currently uses a remote control LHD vehicle for safety and efficiency. These methods cut down on accidental cave-ins and injuries to miners.

- Slusher cut and fill mining to extract ore is used in narrow reef areas. When the areas of ore are six feet or less, high speed machines, or remote control LHD vehicles, cannot access the metals. High pressure water or excessive dilution removes the ore. Slusher cut and fill mining also involves a miner using a slusher or an electric machine with 8-inch scraper bucket. The bucket is attached to a cable drilled into the face of the stope. The machine is behind the ore chute and pulls the bucket forward filling it with ore. Slusher cut and fill methods extract ore from horizontal slices of earth and backfill the mined areas with sand to form the next step.

- Underhand cut and fill mining methods are used to safely mine in various difficult ground conditions. If there is limited access below the ore levels, underhand cut is very affective. In the 1980s hard-rock mining began using cemented mill tailing for backfilling stope cuts. This was to make the cuts in the rock safer. The miners were always working underneath a reinforced cemented backfill. The idea was to safeguard miners in case of a rock burst (http://www.cdc.gov/niosh/mining/userfile s/works/pdfs/ucafm.pdf).

Refining

Removing platinum and palladium from ore requires a complex refining process. After the ore is received at the recovery site a very complex and time-intensive production begins. Mining companies dedicate a significant amount of exploration and mining investment reserves to finding new and better PGM refining technologies.

- Refining separates minerals containing platinum and palladium from base metal and slushes away other impurities. To obtain the most from research, mining and refining dollars, the highest-grade PGM filter cake is made. The process is expensive, detailed and complex. Refinement includes pressure leaching, PGM precipitation and solvent extraction.
- Smelting produces a high grade filter cake that is subjected to a series of complicated chemical processes. The first step is run through a batch grinding process in a closed ball mill. This produces heated slurry. Slurry is cooled and stored in a surge tank. A series of autoclave leach circuits extracts platinum or palladium from the liquid metal composition.

- When conducting chemical reactions under high pressure and temperature, most mining companies tend to rely on aqua regia or a mixture of hydrochloric and nitric acids. These acids dissolve platinum and palladium as well as gold and leave other base metal components as solids. Gold is separated from the solution through solvent extraction and the remaining solution is refined with ammonium chloride. Crude platinum salt is the result. High temperatures create a fine platinum powder, re-dissolved in aqua regia, precipitated with ammonium chloride again and calcined to pure platinum. Palladium is extracted and precipitated with ammonia. Palladium salt is recovered, re-dissolved and formed into palladium salt. The salt is converted to metallic form through a chemical reduction involving formic acid. If you are feeling confused, mining engineers agree the steps involved in extracting platinum and palladium is complex.

Risks

Mining has always been a dangerous occupation. Hundreds of miners die from hard rock mining accidents yearly. Surface mining is usually less dangerous than underground mining, but statistics show that 60 to 70 miners die each year in the non-coal mining industry.

In 2014 a platinum miner was killed in an underground accident near Burgersfort, South Africa. The accident occurred during the mining strikes that have essentially crippled the platinum mining business in South Africa. Latest incident reports report that thirty-two gold mine workers died last month and nine workers lost their lives in a fire was triggered by rock falls in a platinum mine. Illegal miners have been killed in Roodepoort by striking miners (http://www.fin24.com/Companies/Mining/Miner-dies-at-platinum-mine-20140604).

Platinum and palladium are generally mined by opening large underground rooms or stopes. Stoping is practiced in underground mineral mining if the surrounding rock is strong enough to permit drilling blasting and ore removal without caving. Open stoping requires no artificial support and is called room- and- pillar mining. Pillars of ore are left to support the rock over a flat-lying ore body. Cut and fill mining is defined as open stope backfilled with waste materials as ore is removed.

The earliest forms of platinum and palladium mining or stoping mining were carried out with hand tools or fire setting. Later gunpowder was used to blast ore from mountainsides. Starting in the 19th century other types of explosives, power tools and machines were introduced. Stopes filled with tailings frequently collapsed leaving craters on the surface which significantly raised the danger of collapsing earth swallowing men and machines.

Miners must look out for blasting related accidents including:

- Fly-rocks. Most explosive related injuries and fatalities in surface mining happened when workers were struck by rock. They were either too close to the blast point or rocks were thrown farther than expected.
- Premature blasts kill and injure miners. Premature explosions are due to carelessness, accidental percussions, faulty fuses or degenerated explosives.
- Misfires are the partial failure of a blasting charge. The explosion does not go off as planned (National Institute for Occupational Safety and Health).
- Explosive materials can remain in the ground or in the muck pile. These leavings can be triggered by mechanical effects while milling, crushing or digging. Blasts

from these left behind explosives cause deaths and injuries.

Labor disputes are always a risk in mining operations involving different ethnicities and low pay. Volatile tempers lead to beatings, shootings and general mayhem.

Risks in platinum and palladium ore mining like any underground mining endeavor, includes mine blasting-induced seismicity, regions that are seismically active or earthquake like events that collapse mines and trap miners.

Thin ore beds slope downward and cannot be mined with a mechanized approach. Ore beds must be dug out by hand with miners moving along narrow and cramped stopes. The possibility of falls, rock avalanches and blasting for ore on these stopes is high.

Working underground mines is a nasty job for anyone. It is hot and cramped and dangers are around every corner. Rock falls and rock bursts happen frequently because of the pressure. Anything can go wrong at the depth miner's work for platinum and palladium ores.

Why Invest in Platinum and Palladium – Advantages and Disadvantages

Platinum and to a lesser degree, palladium is considered a precious as well as an industrial metal. The primary driving price of platinum and palladium is their industrial use and the largest demand for platinum and palladium is in the automotive industry. The price of platinum and palladium is also dependent on the labor markets in South Africa and Russia. In South Africa labor strikes continue to haunt platinum mining companies. Jobs are being threatened and two platinum mines in South Africa are under consideration for closing due to labor strikes plus pricing issues. Power outages are common and unresolved in many mines causing safety risks. Closure of platinum mines will cause deep cuts in production, loss of jobs and higher prices. Platinum and palladium supplies from mining will drop by 10% in 2014 if any mines are closed. This will drive the cost of platinum up.

Palladium suffers the same market imbalance as platinum – high demand, low inventories and rising prices. Russia is a primary supplier of palladium and stockpiles are quickly depleting. Prices for available supplies are increasing. Also contributing to the higher prices of palladium is the autocatalytic automotive industry. Demand for palladium is expanding as China mandates catalytic systems for all cars driven in the country, and palladium is used in catalytic converters. Additionally there is rising demand for palladium jewelry. Palladium is light in weight and heavier stones can be designed on palladium chains. Asian countries demand high quality palladium for jewelry making which further forces the price per ounce to climb.

The fact that these metals are in demand is the driving force for their popularity in diversified portfolios.

Outlook and Advantages

Investors turn to these precious metals as substitutes for silver and gold. It is true that platinum and palladium are in high demand and their special properties make them perfect for diversifying a precious metals portfolio. PGM has a very different supply-demand consideration which makes them valuable and reduces the risk of a straight-gold portfolio.

Platinum is in high demand in Japan and China for jewelry making. Palladium is used in white gold jewelry and other PGM metals are used in jewelry alloys. This group of metals is also used in industrial applications. Tightening emissions standards in the use of catalytic converters are rapidly leading to higher use of platinum and palladium worldwide. Platinum's high price is a stimulus for finding technologies utilizing palladium for diesel run engines. This makes palladium attractive to investors.

The Quick Guide to Platinum and Palladium

A few years ago platinum prices were nearly 150 percent the price of gold. With a bull run in gold and global recession in platinum, prices have come down to an affordable rate. Industry analysts believe that platinum will continue to rise and the lower prices offer great investment opportunities.

Investment advantage comes from investors who are seeking something with a good store of value in economic times of inflation and eroding currency values. Platinum is not just an investment substitute for gold and silver, but merits a place in any precious metals portfolio. Add platinum and palladium to diversify and hedge your investments.

Metal futures of platinum and palladium are available through commodity brokers. They are excellent investment products and physical shares of platinum and palladium that cover paper stock rapidly joining traditional futures contracts.

- Precious metals can be an actual physical commodity.
- Platinum and palladium are limited commodities. There is not an over abundance of these two precious metals. Like silver, platinum and palladium are two-door metals. They have industrial as well as investment properties. The potential grow compared to bonds, real estate, technologies and bio stocks are low which makes these inventories highly desirable.
- Move into precious metals when the United States economy looks weak and the price is driven up. In others words, buy low and hold.
- Precious metals always have huge value jumps. You can actually get rich if you invest in metals.
- Platinum is highly favored by jewelers. Some jewelers prefer working in platinum versus gold. It is 10 percent more dense than gold and does not need to be

enhanced with other metals. As an interesting note, gold is often combined with platinum to make it durable.

- If you purchased platinum 20 years ago, today in 2014 you would be rich.

Disadvantages of Holding Platinum and Palladium

Prices for platinum and palladium are very volatile. These metals reflect falling as well as raising industrial and investment demand due to the lack of inventories or limited production. The price of platinum and palladium continues to rise and will quickly be beyond the reach of conservative investors.

Gold and silver are known commodities. Platinum is less familiar and palladium is not commonly recognized as a precious metal. There are few platinum coins issued and no palladium coins are available. Gold-minted coins are always in demand and hold a value; not so with platinum.

The Quick Guide to Platinum and Palladium

In a crisis you can sell gold coins or use them as money. This is not the case with palladium or platinum. There are no small denomination platinum coins available, and if you tried to purchase goods and services with platinum coins, you would be denied. Basically, platinum coins will probably not be honored on a day to day basis.

- In the short term, the run up in value of precious metals platinum and palladium has come and gone. If you want to get rich quickly, there are no real opportunities. Value increases on precious metals, but if you have no holdings of precious metals it is not advisable to purchase more holdings when the price is extremely high.
- Precious metals are incredibly volatile investments. It is not uncommon to have a jump of over 50 percent in value in one year. You can also experience a drop of 50 percent in precious metal values.
- Speculators jump into limited precious metals market and seek short-term wealth.

The Quick Guide to Platinum and Palladium

You do need to know the precious metals market inside and out in order to compete with speculators.

- Platinum is more expensive than gold but trades for substantially less. Platinum sells for $150 an ounce less than an ounce of gold.
http://gold-investor.com/article.php/20131120195251223

- Platinum and palladium are small markets. They have the potential for being volatile on the upside and downside in comparison to gold and silver.

- There are only 200 million ounces of platinum as compared to five billion ounces of gold. Mined platinum is only a small fraction of gold and mined palladium enjoys even smaller inventories.

- Currently 40 percent of the world's palladium supply comes from Norilsk in Russia. Platinum and palladium are critical in Japanese industrial uses, but mines in

Russia are under import sanctions by the United Nations due to their activities in the Ukraine. With this problem in mind, will palladium be replaced in the automobile industry as inventories shrink even further?

- Unscrupulous business practices by mining company artificially inflate the prices of platinum and palladium. In 2002 class action suits were filed against Stillwater Mining Company stating they inflated the price of the company's precious metals securities. A court order in 2004 required Stillwater Mining to restate third quarter results. The result was a drop in price for both Stillwater Mining and platinum.

When the automotive industry changed from platinum converters to less costly palladium, the palladium price jumped to more than $1000 an ounce. In order to remain a commodity or in the Future Markets (paper trading) contract holders were required to pay two times the physical price. Sells in the palladium precious market for EFTs essentially stopped.

Investors look at charts to determine the volatility of platinum and palladium and make decisions on investments. Both metals are capable of creating their own price surges even though they rise and fall similar to gold and silver (http://www.silverseek.com/commentary/plati num-today).

Platinum historical price fluctuations

Palladium historical price fluctuations (http://www.silverseek.com/commentary/platin um-today).

Platinum and palladium are evolving into dynamic investment opportunities. An Exchange Traded Fund or ETF tracks an index, commodity or portfolio of assets. As a category, precious metals are valuable as an investment vehicle. It is also possible that physical metals' supplies are being accumulated for use within a given country. This could be part of a strategic reserve to drive the prices up. This alone makes platinum and palladium very attractive to investors.

Buying Platinum and Palladium as an Investment – Coins and Bars

Platinum

There are investors who store metals in physical form. Platinum bars, coins and bullions are available in limited quantities and can be purchased from nationalized and private banks. Physical delivery of platinum is available in weights from 1 gram to 100 grams with 99.5 percent purity. Physically purchasing and holding platinum is still very new in most countries so be careful and get verification or authenticity certificates.

- Several countries have produced platinum coins. The most well-known is the American Platinum Eagle and the Canadian Platinum Maple Leaf. Australian has a platinum Koala coin and the Isle of Man off the coast of Great Britain has issued a platinum Noble coin. If you are lucky you can purchase Chinese platinum Pandas. These are the major coins issued by major government mints. However, if you want a different platinum and palladium bullion, you will need to contact private collectors. At this point in time the American eagle coins are the only platinum coins minted. Foreign governments have ceased issuing platinum coins.
- The front of the coin is an American eagle and the reverse side features the Statue of

Liberty. Most coins are minted in $100 face value increments.

- In the 1990s platinum traded almost at the price of gold. In 1997 the U.S. Mint introduced Platinum Eagles. In 1998, 133,000 one ounce Platinum Eagles were distributed. The prices of Platinum being sold and purchased quickly rose and investors stopped purchasing these coins. In 2003, only 8007 of the coins were minted. Due to demand by investors in 2014, one ounce bullion coins are now available with the current mint date. However it is unsure how long these coins will be available. You can purchase a one ounce American eagle platinum coin for $1,642.00 (http://www.austincoins.com). If you find platinum coins minted in the 19th century and from Russia, you have "gold mine" on your hands. These coins command high premiums and are extremely rare.

- Platinum American eagle coinage is a great investment. Platinum is incredibly rare and there is long-term investment potential from these rare coins.
- Precious metals dealers will sell you platinum and generally in coins. There are also offers on eBay and in local precious metal magazines. Do not purchase any types of precious metal coin from dealers that seem too good to be real or fly by night dealers.
- Note that although banks recognize silver and gold coins, they may not recognize platinum coins. Platinum coins are not as well known as gold and silver and the purchase of platinum coins does affect the platinum market.
- Platinum bullion does not have the interest that gold bullion does. Investors who purchase platinum at high prices do pay smaller markups than gold. Platinum bullion coin buyers who want coins and

bullion with current dates will pay huge premiums.

Platinum plays a very important role on the world market and is a great way to advance a physical precious metal portfolio. Dealers offer very nice array of coins and bars that are almost guaranteed never to lose all of their value. Look for precious metals commodity brokers who offer only the finest quality.

Palladium

Precious metals offer an opportunity to hold real inventory in the form of bullion bars or rounds (coins). Bullion is available for palladium. The purchase price is generally a spot plus basis or the current market spot price plus dealer markup. Dealers can purchase back the bullion, and the price will be the going rate.

- The U.S. Mint released the 142-page Palladium Market Study to allow investors to read about investment opportunities in bullion coins. This report assures investors that palladium coins could be minted and issued at no net cost to taxpayers. Currently there is a drive on to encourage the minting of palladium coins.

- The report emphasized that there is sufficient demand for palladium bullion coins.
- There will not be sufficient demand for U.S. mint palladium numismatic coins, but what coins are minted will be profitable.

Palladium bars and rounds can be bought for $819.50 in various designs. One particular bar features a ballerina en point. You can purchase one of the finest palladium bars on the market depicting Fortuna, the Roman goddess of fortune. If you prefer you can purchase bars in company logos giving the size of the bar and the purity standard (http://www.apmex.com/category/8/palladium -bars-rounds-1-oz-100-oz.)

During the last several years, palladium coins and palladium bullion has become an established precious metal. There is a rise in the demand for palladium and investors are beginning to see the value in coins and bars. Investors are stocking up n palladium products as demand grows. Build a palladium portfolio by choosing coins that are produced from the finest mints in the world. High quality palladium coins and bars are manufactured by Pamp Suisse, Johnson Matthey and Credit Suisse. These bars and coins are refined to .9995 purity. This is a very high standard for the industry.

Diversification and Wealth Building Strategies

Diversifying an investment portfolio is a wise move and will protect your retirement savings. Precious metals can factor into portfolios and represent tangible assets that hedge against market volatility. The amount of precious metals held in your portfolio is totally up to the investor, and should be based on your needs and goals.

When precious metals are discussed most investors are discussing the prices and volatility of gold, silver and platinum. It is possible to buy physical metal and store it in a vault or in a private place. Investors believe this is almost a comfort feeling. They have the tangible assets needed to survive retirement.

You can also purchase precious metal ETFs. ETFs are actually paper certificates whose prices are tied to the current value of the metal. The ETF is ownership of a small amount of a precious metal. When the value of the precious metal raises the value of the EFT also rises.

Some ETFs represent interest. This includes ownership of silver, gold or platinum mines or refiners. These ETFs track with the rise and fall in precious metals. ETFs that are metal interests are less volatile than holding actual product or precious metal ETFs.

Building wealth by using platinum and palladium has appeal as an inflation hedge due to its industrial usages. Heavy industrial demands keep prices of palladium correlated to the automobile industry. The value of the metal is also dependent on emerging markets. Palladium is cheaper than platinum, softer and resistant to rust. Palladium is highly popular for use in dental crowns. Palladium is being tested as a radioactive element and a potential treatment for cancer suffers.

Seeking platinum and palladium to add to your portfolio includes many options. You can buy futures contracts, purchase and hold the physical metal in the form of coins or bars, or investing in mining companies. Purchase platinum and palladium ETFs that track the futures for the metal.

Invest in precious metals and specifically platinum and palladium following this advice:

- If you already have a large portfolio of investments that include many other investments like foreign and domestic stocks, cash, foreign currency and bonds, precious metals is another element of diversification. This would probably be your most volatile asset, but it can provide a hedge against inflation.

- If you do not have a large number of investments, buying precious metals will make your entire portfolio very volatile. You may wake up one morning to find your investments at 50 percent of its original value.
- Investing in real money or physical investments or rare metals gives you immediate and real value. As worldwide currencies fall in value, the only wealth you may have is in your physical holdings of platinum, palladium, gold and silver.

How to Begin

Deciding how much, what type and when to purchase precious metals is overwhelming. Because of advertising, popularity and price stability most investors seek gold shares to add to their investment portfolio. Gold however has seen volatile trading starting in 2013. Gold is not as popular as it was in the early 2000s and now investors are looking at other commodities to add to their wealth building strategies.

Popular precious metals choices are now including palladium and platinum. Both metals are dominated by South African mining and production. Due to labor issues, utility problems and government issues the platinum and palladium industry is experiencing shutdowns and profit losses. Anglo American, the world's largest platinum producer, posted a $753 million loss for 2012. The inability to close loss-generating mines in South Africa is a big reason platinum and palladium prices fail to meet the cost of production.

Predictions by market analysts, state since platinum and palladium are in small supply and there are industry demands, demand issues and both precious metals are becoming highly attractive in investment portfolios.

Unlike gold, platinum and palladium focus on industrial uses. They take their pricing volatility from the economy. The global economy is improving and people are purchasing more automobiles. The key driver of platinum and palladium is catalytic converts and the demand for stringent automobile regulations.

Increased demand and reduced supply drive up platinum and palladium prices. Investors need to cycle investing into these PGMs for the next few years. Consider bullion purchases at local coin dealerships, online retailers and consider ETFs as a part of your investment portfolio.

- Seek brokers who provide future contracts.
- Physically purchase and hold the metal in the form of coins or bars.
- Purchase stocks of companies that mine platinum and palladium.

- Purchase platinum and palladium ETFs that are physically backed up by metals held in vaults.

The lesser known precious metals platinum and palladium are the tickets to portfolio diversification. These metals have soared in value in the past ten years. They are considered new metals with a recognition date in the 1800s. When gold soars in price platinum and palladium receive an upsurge. Most precious metals move together. Platinum generally follows the price of gold and can sell at a premium.

- Investors suggest investing in gold and silver before platinum and palladium. Statements by investors include, "Platinum and palladium aren't for everyone because markets are smaller. They're nicer to have rather than need. Investors go on to say that these coveted metals for use in catalytic converters in cars can be a huge help in diversifying your portfolio and a good hedge against financial volatility.

- Check out platinum and palladium through a precious metal broker. An expert in the metal commodities will give you advice on the best times to buy and sell.
- Investors advise you hold metals certificates or physical stores for at least three years.
- Platinum and palladium should never be more than 5 percent of your portfolio. Gold and silver should be at least 10 percent. Markets for platinum and palladium are small and trading is limited.
- Set up a target price when selling. Prices should not drive your investment strategies. Holding precious metals in a portfolio requires almost an emotional attachment.
- Platinum is far rarer than gold and limited supplies mean wildly fluctuating prices. In 2008 platinum sold at $2,252 per ounce but plummeted to $794 in the same year.

Supply issues caused a higher price, but when the problem was fixed, the price dropped. Platinum has never again reached such an all-time high price.

- Invest in bullion coins or coins that are minted specifically for investors. Hold onto the coins and stop worrying about the ups and downs of the market. Look for U.S. mint-issued American eagle platinum coins. They can be purchased at banks, directly from the U.S. Mint or from brokerage firms. You can also purchase platinum and palladium bullion at major coin dealers. You can surf the U.S Mint website for a list of authorized dealers.
- Platinum futures contracts are not as liquid as gold and silver and the market is prone to erratic price movement.
- Prices of platinum typically rise during inflation.
- These precious metals are considered a "safe-haven" investment. When there is

political or economic instability, platinum prices typically rise.

- Buying platinum bullion is a popular option.
- Invest in precious metals by buying futures contracts on exchange. This provides leverage, but is higher risk. You do not need to physically store platinum since this type of investment is electronic and regulated by the exchanges, NFA and CFTC.
- Stocks of mining companies who publicly trade platinum are good investments.
- Mutual funds that invest in stocks involved in precious metals are good papers to hold in investment.

Investing in precious metals has the reputation of never being worth zero. Metals will retain their intrinsic value regardless of economic circumstances. Diverse your investments by holding shares in mining companies, ETF paper that are backed by bullion, and actual physical stores of precious metals. Look for antique coins that are worth more than their meltdown value.

The inventories of platinum and palladium are constantly changed due to sales by large investors and active mining. Do research before buying platinum and palladium. You will need safe place to store coins or bullion and watch the market for volatility in price. The less liquid platinum and palladium market means coins and bullion are harder to cash in. Before purchasing bullion or coins, check out the dealer's buy back policy.

Storage

Investors are seeking direct ownership of physical precious metals including platinum and palladium. Companies specializing in storage also offer sourcing, transporting, buying and storing your precious metal investments. Storage facilities do set minimums and carry high insurance. Vaults of most third party precious metal storages facilities are located in tax-free zones and bonded warehouses. This helps to avoid duties and taxes.

There are companies created to invest and hold all of its assets in physical platinum and palladium bullion. The purpose is to provide secure and convenient investment alternatives for investors who want to own physical platinum and palladium bullion without the inconvenience of holding it in house. These companies do not speculate with regard to short-term change in prices; they only hold the precious metals in vaults and charge a storage fee.

- Viable investment companies hold and store platinum and palladium at secure third party storage locations in different countries. Further security measures insist physical bullion is subject to inspection on a rotating basis and audits are randomly performed.

- Third party storage facilities are convenient and provide investors with access to their physical platinum and palladium bullion whenever needed.
- Storage facilities are cost effective. Most storage firms charge management fee per year.

Most third-party storage firms also provide storage facilities for gold, silver, diamonds and other luxury goods. It is your choice where you store your precious metals. Vaults are located all over the world and primarily in Singapore, London, New York, Hong Kong, Shanghai, Zurich and Bangkok. You can have vaults the size of safety deposit boxes up to entire dedicated rooms customized to keep your physical luxury items safe.

Conclusion

Platinum is unique. The properties in platinum make it valuable in many industries.

- The automobile industry looks for platinum for exhaust catalyst converters. These converters convert emissions to non-toxic substances. Regulations require new cars be manufactured with catalytic converters. The automobile industry uses about a third of platinum stores.
- Platinum is highly sought after for use in jewelry. Platinum is strong, lasts for years, and is tarnish resistant and gorgeous when molded into wedding and engagement rings. Platinum has been a popular metal for precious jewelry since the 18th century. Some archeologists state that platinum was also used in ancient Egypt for jewelry fit for the pharaohs.
- Canada, Australia, Isle of Man, China and the U.S. mint platinum coins for investment purposes. Swiss companies are

able to produce pure platinum bars and coins at 99.95 percent pure. Platinum availability in coins and bars can be purchased up to one ounce.

Palladium has strong demand for use in internal combustion engines an autocatalysts. Autocatalysts convert 90 percent of harmful emissions – hydrocarbons, carbon monoxide and nitrogen oxides – into nitrogen, water vapor and carbon dioxide and palladium's properties directly contribute to this transformation.

- Palladium is in high demand for use in electronics. Chemical stability and electrical conductively make palladium a durable alternative to gold for electronic components.
- Dentistry uses palladium alloy for dental crows and bridges. Palladium is highly used in radioactive form in the medical industry for cancer treatments.

- Palladium used in refining nitric acid and is useful in developing raw materials for nylon and rubber commodities.
- Petroleum refineries use palladium.
- Current experiments using palladium as s catalyst for use in removing toxic substances from groundwater.
- Palladium is a metal sought after in jewelry production for its strength and lightness plus durability.

Consider palladium as an investment. Make sure your palladium dealer will buy back your bullion at current market price if you ever need to sell quickly.

The interest in investing in platinum and palladium is still low. Although platinum and palladium are considered precious metals because they have a store of value, they are industrial metals with known properties in the electronics, automobile, dentistry and pharmaceutical industries. Some investors devalue these precious metals due to these industrial demands. Platinum and palladium are not widely recognized as investments. Their futures markets are sparingly traded and the available ETFs are highly liquid.

Investors who speculate in gold and silver mines find platinum and palladium mining companies poor investments. South Africa and Russia, the two largest producers, have labor issues and unstable economies. Investment specialists point out that North American mining companies fare no better. The largest companies have lost value and scaled back their mining and refining abilities. This does not fare well for platinum and palladium stocks.

Consider the supplies of platinum and palladium. Supplies are very limited, the risk of mining these metals is tremendous, and reserves of these precious metals are 50 percent lower than gold reserves. This gives the investor the assumption that both metals should trade high. Platinum and palladium have unique industrial applications. Look to the old adage, "buy low and sell high." Platinum and palladium definitely have this potential. You can buy physical coin bullion of platinum from government mints, but the easiest way to buy share is to utilize an ETF. Research listed companies like Physical Platinum Trust (listed on ASDAQ), and ETF Securities Physical palladium (listed on the NYSE).

Do avoid these precious metals if your portfolio is small and investments are low in number. Having shares of platinum and palladium will cause your investment package to be volatile and unstable. Diversify your investment portfolio. Hold 5 percent of your assets in platinum and palladium and keep your gold and silver investments at 10 percent. Holding precious metals gives you a hedge against market volatility. Savvy investors know that market demand equals strength.

Warning: Your capital is at risk when you invest in platinum and palladium - you can lose some or all of your money, so never risk more than you can afford to lose. Always seek professional advice if you are unsure about the suitability of any investment. Past performance is not a reliable indicator of future results.

Every attempt has been made to provide accurate, up to date and reliable complete information, no warranties of any kind are expressed or implied. Readers acknowledge that the author is not engaging in rendering legal, financial or professional advice.

The reader agrees that under no circumstances are we responsible for any losses, direct or indirect, which are incurred as a result of use of the information contained within this book, including – but not limited to errors, omissions, or inaccuracies.

Check Out Other Books:

Investing in Gold and Silver Bullion - The Ultimate Safe Haven Investments

Nigerian Stock Market Investment: 2 Books with Bonus Content

The Dividend Millionaire: Investing for Income and Winning in the Stock Market

Economic Crisis: Surviving Global Currency Collapse - Safeguard Your Financial Future with Silver and Gold

Passionate about Stock Investing: The Quick Guide to Investing in the Stock Market

Guide to Investing in the Nigerian Stock Market

Building Wealth with Dividend Stocks in the Nigerian Stock Market (Dividends - Stocks Secret Weapon)

Beginners Basic Guide to Investing in Gold and Silver Boxed Set

Beginners Basic Guide to Stock Market Investment Boxed Set

Taming the Tongue: The Power of Spoken Words

Beginners Quick Guide to Passive Income:
Learn Proven Ways to Earn Extra Income in
the Cyber World

Christian Living: 2 Books with Bonus Content

Bitcoin and Digital Currency for Beginners:
The Basic Little Guide

If you would like to share this book with another person, please purchase an additional copy for each recipient. Thank you for respecting the hard work of this author.

Thank you for downloading the book,
Precious Metals Investing for Beginners: The
Quick Guide to Platinum and Palladium.

The Quick Guide to Platinum and Palladium

The Quick Guide to Platinum and Palladium

www.ingramcontent.com/pod-product-compliance
Lightning Source LLC
Chambersburg PA
CBHW070933180526
45168CB00003B/1055